Sports Day
at
Sandy Bay

Kim and Tim like to help.

Kim and Tim
help Miss Sim.

Kim and Tim help a lot.

3

Can we help?

Pen and Ben like to help.

Pen and Ben help Jack.

Pen and Ben help a lot.

5

Rob and Spot help to fix the tent.

Rob and Spot help to get the mugs and jugs.

It is hot.
The sun is hot.

Ali and his dad
get the big mats.
Ali and his dad
get hot!

The mums and dads and Gran sit down.

Can Spot run?
Miss Sim, can Spot run?

Miss Sim, Miss Sim, let Spot run.

No Rob, no! Sit down!

We run. Pen wins.

We hop. Ben wins.

We skip. Ali wins.

We jump. Rob wins.

Jack's fat cat jumps
off his lap.
She runs and runs!
Mum's pug jumps
off the rug.

He runs and runs!

Spot runs and runs!

Spot wins!